GIVING
THAT MATTERS
to God

A Fresh Look at Christian Stewardship for You and Your Church

GIVING
THAT MATTERS

to God

WENDELL VAN GUNST AND BETSY ARKEMA

XULON PRESS

Xulon Press
2301 Lucien Way #415
Maitland, FL 32751
407.339.4217
www.xulonpress.com

© 2021 by Wendell Van Gunst and Betsy Arkema

All rights reserved solely by the author. The author guarantees all contents are original and do not infringe upon the legal rights of any other person or work. No part of this book may be reproduced in any form without the permission of the author. The views expressed in this book are not necessarily those of the publisher.

Unless otherwise indicated, Scripture quotations taken from the Holy Bible, New International Version (NIV). Copyright © 1973, 1978, 1984, 2011 by Biblica, Inc.™. Used by permission. All rights reserved.

Printed in the United States of America.

Paperback ISBN-13: 978-1-6628-0782-4
eBook ISBN-13: 978-1-6628-0783-1

Table of Contents

Introduction.................................. vii

Chapter 1: Follower or Believer, Does it Matter?....1

Chapter 2: Knowing Christ's Mission
               is What Matters....................15

Chapter 3: What is the Matter With My Giving?...33

Chapter 4: Giving That Matters 45

Chapter 5: A Church That Matters to God 59

Chapter 6: Can Your Church Matter?............81

Chapter 7: Risk Takers Matter to God 93

Conclusion 107

Introduction

My daughter and I have been thinking about this Bible study for quite a long time. It has been a great time of challenging discussions on a subject we both feel deeply about: Christian stewardship. It's hard to imagine another subject with the same potential effect on how we live out Jesus' command to "go and make disciples of all nations" (Matt. 26:19). If the average Christian gives about 3 percent of their income to Christian causes, can you imagine the effect even a 1 percent increase would have on the world? Making that happen with just this study guide seems unlikely, but Ephesians 3:20 reminds us that nothing is impossible with God.

I have had the privilege to speak about stewardship in many churches. I have found that concerns about the local church budget often keep pastors from candidly talking about the concern Jesus expected his followers to have for His people who are lost and hurting around the world. Pastors and teachers seem more likely to challenge us to obey the Ten Commandments than the

Great Commission. This Bible study is designed to help you explore and understand the full scope of Jesus' final instructions, especially as they relate to your finances.

From Jesus' teachings throughout the gospels, we must conclude that how we use our money can get in the way of becoming the type of follower He wanted. We know that following Jesus involves much more than money, but we also believe we need to be aware of how concerned Jesus was with money and wealth. His warning that "it is easier for a camel to go through the eye of a needle than for someone who is rich to enter the kingdom of God" (Mark 10:25) should give us all pause. Jesus portrays an impossible picture since no one has ever seen a camel that had any hope of getting through the eye of a needle. On the other hand, we cannot ignore Jesus' substantial promises to those who are willing to give sacrificially to God's work. To think that so many of us who profess to be Christ followers may be missing out on the blessings that God wants to give us would seem to be reason enough to spend some time working through this study.

While most stewardship education seems to be directed only toward individual Christ followers, this study also intends to highlight the church's clear responsibility to talk about Christian stewardship as a body—not just through its teaching, but by setting an example. We hope this study will cause you to ask, "What does my level of stewardship say about me as a Christ follower?"

Introduction

as well as, "What is the real focus of my church's ministry?" We think some of the questions we raise in this study will be ones you have not faced before. It is our hope and prayer that you will face these questions with an open mind.

One of my concerns when writing about this subject is that readers will have the impression that I believe my own stewardship meets Jesus' standards. Nothing could be further from the truth.

This study is born out of a very real and personal struggle with this difficult subject—one that I still learn and pray about every day.

Our prayer for you is that something in this study will change your giving habits. Our hope is that this study will spark honest and deep discussions about the challenges of stewardship that we all face in our personal lives and in the churches we are part of. We are convinced that, if it does, you will experience more of God's promised blessings and become a real part of changing the world God cares so much about. Reading and learning and studying without change or action is empty. So as you use this study guide, we will be praying that God will inspire you to take those first difficult steps toward real change. We have all the confidence and trust that our God is and will be at work. Nothing is impossible for our God, who has promised to walk beside us every step of the way.

—Wendell Van Gunst

"No one who puts a hand to the plow and looks back is fit for service in the kingdom of God."
—Luke 9:62

LESSON 1

FOLLOWER OR BELIEVER: DOES IT MATTER?

We begin this study in Luke 9:62 (written above). The picture of plowing that Jesus uses here is somewhat surprising. It is a picture that only a farmer could truly understand. Any farmer who has ever plowed a field knows the importance of having straight furrows. To that end, when they start across the field they find a point to aim for, a tree, a fence post, something that doesn't move that they can focus on. Once headed across the field with the plow, every farmer also knows (probably from experience) that if they take their eyes off that one immoveable target and look back their furrow will end up crooked. Jesus uses these simple words in Luke to teach us an important lesson about following Him: If you've decided to follow Him - keep your eyes fixed on Him, the one thing that will not move, and don't look back, don't question your choice. Go all in with your eyes firmly fixed on Jesus. With this lesson in mind, we begin this book on stewardship.

A familiar song sung by many Christians is "I Have Decided to Follow Jesus." Have you ever really thought about the lyrics to this song? Particularly, the word, "follow". What do you think the writer of this song was trying to say by using this word, follow? When you sing this song, what do you mean when you sing, "I have decided to <u>follow</u> Jesus"? Do you think the title and lyrics of this song accurately describe most Christians today? What if the title was "I Have Decided to <u>Believe</u> in Jesus"? Which of these titles do you think best describes most Christians' understanding of their relationship with Jesus? Would they describe themselves as believers or followers?

Most of us are familiar with John 3:16: "For God so loved the world that he gave his one and only Son, that whoever believes in him shall not perish but have eternal life." This verse tells us that believing is enough, and we do not want to take anything away from this fundamental principle.. But perhaps the word "believe" should be clarified. What do I mean when I say, "I believe"? It is realistic to think that someone could say, "I believe Jesus was a real person who came to earth, did miracles, died, and rose again," but I don't think this is all that is meant in John 3:16.

The rest of John 3 tells us that belief requires not only the conviction that Jesus existed and was who He said He was. It must also include a recognition on the part of the believer that this salvation and promise of eternal life is available *only through Jesus*. Once believers have come to this point - acknowledging who Jesus is and why they need him - then they are saved and have access to the promised eternal life. But then what? How does this new belief impact them? Does it alter the course of their lives? What is the next step?

As Jesus began his ministry on earth, what did He ask of people? When Jesus called His disciples, He asked them to "follow" Him. Consider these words of Jesus: "Whoever does not take up their cross and follow me is not worthy of me" (Matt. 10:38). What did Jesus mean by "follow"? Is this different from simple belief?

In today's world we follow a lot of things. We follow people on Facebook, Twitter, and Instagram. We follow our favorite sports teams, both professional and collegiate. We follow our favorite musicians and bands. We follow our kids in their sports or the concerts and plays they're involved in. As Christians, we profess to be followers of Jesus Christ. But do we really understand what it means to follow Jesus? Is it the same as following all these other things, or is it somehow different? In this first chapter, we're going to look closely at what exactly it means to be a Christ-follower.

As Jesus was preparing to begin His ministry here on earth, He called twelve men to come and follow Him. The Bible describes some of those conversations:

> **Matt. 4:18–22** "As Jesus was walking beside the Sea of Galilee, he saw two brothers, Simon called Peter and his brother Andrew. They were casting a net into the lake, for they were fishermen. "Come, follow me," Jesus said, "and I will send you out to fish for people." At once they left their nets and followed him.
>
> Going on from there, he saw two other brothers, James son of Zebedee and his brother John. They were in a boat with their father Zebedee, preparing their nets. Jesus called them, and immediately they left the boat and their father and followed him"

What do you think Jesus was asking these men to do when He said, "Come, follow me"? Was it simply to walk behind Him as he traveled and taught? To observe Him like a reporter? Or to leave their livelihoods to learn and be trained by Jesus to carry on what He would begin?

I suppose you could argue that any of these could be the answer, but if you had to choose just one, I think the last option is the obvious choice. Jesus wasn't just looking for companions or even biographers. He was looking to teach and train these men to "fish for people." As we look further in the story of Jesus, we see He had more conversations about this idea of following Him. Let's look at some of these conversations to help us understand a bit more about what Jesus meant.

In Matthew 10, Jesus says,

> "Anyone who loves their father or mother more than me is not worthy of me; anyone who loves their son or daughter more than me is not worthy of me. Whoever does not take up their cross and follow me is not worthy of me" Matthew 10:37-38

And in Luke 9:57–62, we read:

> As they were walking along the road, a man said to him, "I will follow you wherever you go." Jesus "Foxes have dens and birds have nests, but the Son of Man has no place to lay his head."
>
> He said to another man, "Follow me." But he replied, "Lord, first let me go and bury my father." Jesus said to him, "Let the dead bury their own dead, but you go and proclaim the kingdom of God." Still another said "I will follow you, Lord; but first let me go back and say goodbye to my family." Jesus replied "No one who puts a hand to the plow and looks back is fit for service in the kingdom of God."

- List the things Jesus ranks as second to following Him.

- What do you think Jesus is suggesting by setting up these standards for following Him?

- Jesus says His followers must be willing to give up important things for Him. Have you ever given up anything to follow Jesus? Has being a follower of Jesus cost you anything?

- The requests made by the people who asked to first go and bury their father or to say goodbye to their family seem reasonable. Why do you think Jesus said no? What does Jesus' answer tell us?

In the Matthew passage, Jesus says His followers must be willing to "take up their cross." Why would Jesus use the word "cross" here? Certainly He's not expecting you to carry around a literal cross, so what might this "cross" that we're supposed to "take up" symbolize? In Jesus' time, crucifixions were one of the ways the Roman government carried out capital punishment. This extremely cruel and humiliating punishment was a powerful deterrent to those who might choose to rise up against Rome. The process always started with a severe flogging, resulting in tremendous blood loss and bringing the convicted person close to death. Then the person would be forced to carry the cross they would be crucified on out to the crucifixion site. The crossbeam would be tied to the person's wrists and carried across his back. At this point there is no turning back for the convicted. There is no hope of a last-ditch effort to stay this execution. The convicted person is well on their way to death and certainly resigned to it.

Jesus, too, picked up His cross and carried it, knowing that waiting for Him at the end of this road was a torturous and agonizing death. But He also knew that this road, this death, would bring abundant and eternal life to everyone who would follow Him. This road, this death, was necessary to bring life.

When Jesus asks us to take up our crosses and follow Him, he's asking us to come to terms with the fact that this path does not lead to security, comfort, protection, or safety. This path goes in a direction the world will never understand. On this path there will be sacrifice. But what is this sacrifice that we as Christ-followers must be willing to accept?

One of the most difficult sacrifices is to fully acknowledge that everything I have belongs to God. Understanding that I'm just a manager of God's gifts and not the owner. Surrendering my own desires and seeking what God wants instead. Jesus promises that if we *are* willing to put aside what we want to follow Him, we will know the life God has planned for us. The path Jesus asks us to walk is not the wide and easy path. The good news is that, just as Jesus' story didn't end at the cross, our story isn't finished at the end of our earthly path. Jesus promises that following His path will end with the gift of eternal life with Him.

In the following verses, and in many others, Jesus is clear about the seriousness of His call to follow Him. He asks for our whole selves—not just the parts that are easy, convenient, or socially acceptable to sacrifice. In fact, Jesus says the exact opposite: following Him is going to be difficult and unpopular.

It must be clear that Jesus has expectations of His followers that go beyond just believing. Jesus wants people who are believers, but He expects all of us to act on that faith. When He called those first disciples He was clear about His intention to make them "fishers of people." Do you think Jesus would have accepted disciples who said they'd be willing to learn, but that taking action was not for them? In all these passages Jesus clearly expects action from believers. His final command to "go and make disciples" surely was also meant for all of us who call ourselves believers. Jesus expects our believing to result in action. That action may be different for each of us, but it isn't optional.

In Matthew 7:13–14 Jesus cautions us:

> Enter through the narrow gate. For wide is the gate and broad is the road that leads to destruction, and many enter through it. But small is the gate and narrow the road that leads to life, and only a few find it.

In Romans 12:1–2, Paul counsels Christ-followers:

> Therefore, I urge you, brothers and sisters, in view of God's mercy, to offer your bodies as a living sacrifice, holy and pleasing to God—this is your true and proper worship. Do not conform to the pattern of this world, but be transformed by the renewing of your mind. Then you will be able to test and approve what God's will is—his good, pleasing and perfect will.

- Why do you think the gate that leads to destruction is wide and the road that leads to life is narrow? If a road leads to life, why will so few find the narrow road? Do Jesus' words that few will find the right path concern you?

- In Romans 12, Paul uses the phrase "offer your bodies as a living sacrifice." What do you think a living sacrifice is? What might a living sacrifice look like? How would you recognize someone who is a living sacrifice? Do you think this phrase would have sounded strange to Roman Christians? What kinds of sacrifices were they accustomed to seeing?

- Paul also says in Romans 12, "Do not conform to the pattern of this world." What issues do you think Paul was most concerned about here? Paul implies that the pattern of the world is not consistent with the pattern of Jesus. What are some of the differences between these two patterns?

- If you agree there is a difference between believing in Jesus and following Jesus, how would you describe that difference? How important is this difference?

- Can a Christian be a believer and not a follower? Can you be a follower and not a believer? Why or why not?

- Imagine Jesus sitting with you now and asking, "Are you a believer or a follower of mine?" How would you answer him?

If you had to acknowledge today that you're probably more a believer than a follower of Jesus, we don't think you're alone. It seems very possible that sitting in our church pews on Sunday and among our circles of Christian friends there may be many who are believers but have not made the transition to being followers. The good news, however, is that Jesus wants to help us become followers. It's what He did for his disciples,

His friends, and even His brothers. He taught them and showed them what following Him really means, and He challenged them to do the same. Jesus' words and actions are for us too—and not only that, but in Acts 1:8, Jesus promises more: "You will receive power when the Holy Spirit comes on you; and you will be my witnesses in Jerusalem, and in all Judea and Samaria, and to the ends of the earth." When Jesus went back to heaven to be with his Father, the Holy Spirit was sent here to live in our hearts, to guide us, to teach us, to admonish us, and to develop us as followers of Jesus.

- It's apparent from what Jesus taught His disciples that following him is not an easy thing to do. It requires a high level of commitment. Why do you think Jesus asks for this? Why is this so important?

We know it won't be easy, but we also know that we don't walk down this path alone. Just before Jesus went back to heaven, as part of His final words to his followers, He said, "Surely I am with you always, to the very end of the age" (Matt. 28:20). Jesus wants us to be His followers, and He promises to help us along the way. So where do we start? We'll learn that in the next chapter. But first we have two final questions.

- If you find yourself to be more of a believer than a follower, what would you need to do or change to become a follower of Jesus?

- If Jesus stopped by your home or workplace today and said, "Come, follow me," how would your response compare to that of the disciples? In our lesson the people came to Jesus with what seemed like very reasonable requests, saying things like "Let me first go and bury my father," or "Let me first go and say goodbye to my family." But Jesus told them no. What might be your seemingly reasonable request to Jesus? What would you want to do first?

"For God so loved the world that he gave his one and only Son, that whoever believes in him shall not not perish but have eternal life."
—John 3:16

LESSON 2

KNOWING CHRIST'S MISSION IS WHAT MATTERS

So you want to be a follower of Jesus. Great! Wait—are you really sure?

We discussed in the first lesson that following Jesus means being a living sacrifice, and it means more than just being a believer. Jesus wants real followers. But we have busy lives. We must pay loving attention to our spouses, our kids, and our jobs, and we have hobbies and other responsibilities. So if I want to be one of those followers of Jesus and not just a believer, what does that mean for me—today, tomorrow, next week, next month, next year? Is being a follower going to change my day-to-day life, and if so, how?

In the first lesson we came to understand that Jesus' early followers did not just watch what Jesus was doing. They followed so they could not only <u>see</u> what Jesus was doing but more importantly <u>learn</u> from Jesus every day. By doing this they were able to see and experience what really mattered to Jesus. Listening to Jesus' parables and watching Him interact with people must have challenged their own ideas and traditions. To be that kind of follower, we need to take our own agendas, schedules, plans, and hopes and replace them with the agenda of Jesus, the person we've committed to following. The next step, then, is to understand what Jesus' agenda was and is today.

Jesus called His first followers by saying, "Come, follow me, and I will send you out to fish for people" (Matt. 4:19). It's important to understand why Jesus would use these particular words. He could have said "Come, follow me, and I will show you how I will change the world," or "Come, follow me, and I will teach you all about your heavenly Father," or "Come, follow me, and you will learn to do amazing things." So why did Jesus choose these words—"I will send you out"—to call those original followers?

Until Christ came, God chose to work in this world through the nation of Israel. They were God's chosen people, and their coming Messiah would bring about the redemption of the whole world. All of Israel looked forward to his coming. Yet the religious leaders who were the most knowledgeable about the prophecies and scriptures, who had been watching for signs of the coming of the Messiah for generations—those leaders rejected Jesus. They hung Him on a cross and did everything within their power to stamp out His ministry.

Jesus was fully aware of this. He knew what was going to happen as He began and fulfilled His ministry. Using the religious establishment to tell a lost world that there was now a way out of the mess of sin would seem to make the most sense. But Jesus knew that the leaders would instead be the ones who would kill Him, the very Messiah they were looking for. So how could Jesus get his message out to the world? Surely He had this in mind when He called those first disciples with those simple but important words: "Come, follow me, and I will send you out to fish for people." This is the call for all those who would follow Jesus. He wants you to be a fisher of people. God so loved the world that God sent God's son, Jesus, who wants you and me, His followers, to proclaim God's love to a lost and hurting world.

Some of the disciples that He called were just simple fishermen. These men became the focus of

Jesus' teaching on earth. For three years He did with them some of what we still do in the church today: they worshiped together, prayed together, Jesus taught them about His kingdom, and then He sent them out to practice what they had learned. There was a clear purpose to Jesus' teaching, and there was no question about the expected outcome: to develop them into fishers of people.

It's important to notice that these twelve men spent three years being with and learning from Jesus. They witnessed His death and resurrection. And then Jesus ended His earthly ministry by telling them to go and do what He'd been training them to do: to tell the world about who He was and what He did. That is still the essence of His call to the church today. Jesus calls the church not to a lifelong adult education program, but to develop His followers into active ministers, sharing the gospel and helping the hurting. That is what following Jesus was—and still is—all about. These fishers of people did not need theological degrees. The message they brought was simple: Jesus is alive, and He offers forgiveness, a new life, and a new future to all who will believe and follow Him.

In 2 Corinthians 5:17-20, Paul lays out what he believes is the mission of every Christ follower and the church. These verses are the heart of this chapter and will be the basis for the rest of our discussion. Paul's words are very clear about the work that God expects from His followers and from His church.

> [17]Therefore, if anyone is in Christ, the new creation has come: The old has gone, the new is here!

> [18]All this is from God, who reconciled us to himself through Christ and gave us the ministry of reconciliation: [19]that God was reconciling the world to himself in Christ, not counting people's sins against them. And he has committed to us the message of reconciliation.

> [20]We are therefore Christ's ambassadors, as though God were making his appeal through us. We implore you on Christ's behalf: Be reconciled to God.

The message and meaning in these verses is critical to our discussion. In order to grasp the full impact of this passage, we are going to study it in three different sections. The first section is verse 17.

> 2 Corinthians 5:17-20 "Therefore, if anyone is in Christ, the new creation has come. The old has gone, the new is here!"

Giving that Matters to God

It's hard to imagine any verse in the Bible that should impact Christ-followers more than this verse. Paul is saying here that the gospel <u>really</u> matters. He thought it mattered so much that this truth should affect every aspect of people's lives. How much does the gospel really matter to you? How much does it really affect your day-to-day life? How you answer this question will have a tremendous effect on how you follow Jesus, and nothing will impact what your following Jesus looks like more.

Paul says in this verse that if you are in Christ—if you are a follower of Jesus—you are a new creation! Let that sink in for a minute. The old parts, the broken parts, the damaged, the wounded, the hurt—they are all gone! By His sacrifice, Jesus makes you new! Sin does not control you any longer. Romans 3:21 says, "But now apart from the law the righteousness of God has been made known." In other words, the power of sin has been broken, and the gift of eternal life is now yours.

To put this in context, let me share this story. Recently we finally gave in to the fact that we needed new appliances in our kitchen. Our dishwasher had just plain quit working; the water wouldn't drain after the wash cycle, so it was useless. Our refrigerator would slowly leak water into the space below the fruit and vegetable drawers. Over time the water would overflow and make a puddle on the kitchen floor. The handles were so worn they weren't white anymore, and the freezer's ice maker had long since given up. Our stove—well, that was becoming a real hazard. The front right burner would randomly heat up to high no matter what the dial was set to. I don't know how many times we ruined not only supper, but pots and pans as well. This winter we finally took the plunge and purchased all new appliances.

Comparing ourselves as a new creation to a new set of Maytag appliances is a bit of a stretch, I know. But we were ridiculously excited about those new appliances. They actually worked! When we pushed the buttons, the right burner heated up to the right temperature, the water drained when it was supposed to, and it didn't drain where it wasn't supposed to. All the quirks and flaws and dangers of the old were replaced with the trustworthy, dependable, and productive qualities of the new. We didn't have to worry about all those things that didn't work right anymore. We didn't have to keep checking to make sure nothing was burning, leaking, or malfunctioning. Those troubles were gone—they got carried away to the dump, never to be seen again!

Now, if anyone can be that excited about appliances that actually work, how much more should the freedom from sin and the assurance of an eternal life in heaven with a God who loves me more than I can even comprehend transform my every moment! We still walk into the kitchen in the morning and love our new appliances. Do I wake up every morning and marvel at my

God, who saved me and makes me new? Have I stopped worrying about my broken and faulty past and begun to revel in the newness that is my present and future? Do I go throughout my day feeling rescued and new? I should—I absolutely should!

Because of Jesus, we are *new*. The old is gone. The gospel really does matter. It changes absolutely everything. It forever changes the way we look at our past, the way we face today, and the way we see our future. One of the fundamental beliefs of a Christ-follower is that this gospel is the only way to eternal life. This gospel truly is a life-and-death issue that affects all of eternity and every person's eternal destiny. That's a big deal! Most Christians know that in their head, but do we really know that truth in our hearts? If we did—if we lived every day convicted of the truth that that Jesus came here to live among us, to teach and love people, to suffer and die for people, to conquer death—then don't you think it would affect what we do, what we say, and even how we spend our money? The idea that the gospel of Jesus Christ matters to everyone should motivate everything we do. It should drive the conversations I have with people, where I spend my time, and how I spend my money. What more valuable thing could there be to spend our time and money on than people's eternity? And if you really believe people's eternal destiny depends on their hearing and responding to the gospel, then you will share the gospel wherever and however you can.

That's what happened to Paul. In Acts 26, Paul stands before King Agrippa as a prisoner, defending the gospel that he has been teaching. You can feel Paul's passion as he describes to the king how the gospel of Jesus Christ changed his life. He explains to King Agrippa that he wanted nothing to do with this message at first. In fact, he did everything in his power to stamp it out, including putting Christians in jail and consenting to their death. But God stopped Paul on his way to Damascus, and everything changed. It was this event, this lightbulb moment, that turned Paul into a dynamic leader of the church. We don't all have lightbulb moments as big and dramatic as Paul's, but the before and after are the same. We were trapped in our sin with no hope of getting out on our own. God comes in and shows us how much He loves us and what He was willing to do to get us back. That changes everything.

Paul's lightbulb moment led him to say in 1 Corinthians 9:16, "Woe to me if I do not preach the gospel!" Once Paul got a taste of this new reality, he just couldn't keep it to himself. This realization of what God had done for him and for every other person walking on this planet with him changed the entire direction of his life. His life was no longer about himself; it had to be about making sure people knew what God had shown him. He had to make sure he shared this gospel message with as many people as possible no matter his circumstances, no matter the cost, no matter what it took. If the gospel had this kind of effect on Paul, shouldn't it have the same effect on us? Yes—if the gospel really matters to us.

I once heard a pastor remember a time he attended a service at the Vietnam Veterans Memorial. He noticed a reporter interviewing a person who had traveled a long distance to attend the service that day. The reporter, surprised at how far this man had come to attend the service, asked him why it was so important for him to be there. The veteran walked over to the wall and traced with his fingers the letters of another man's name engraved there. Through tears, the veteran explained that this man had given his life for him. "That's why I came," he said, "and there is nothing I wouldn't do to show my gratitude for giving up his life to save mine."

Every time we take communion we are saying what that veteran said about his friend. Every time we take the bread and cup it's like we're tracing the name of Jesus with our finger. We're saying that there is a person named Jesus Christ who gave up His life for me. What do we do in response to that? What *should* we do? Are we willing to be like that veteran and say, "There is nothing I wouldn't do to show my gratitude for what He did for me"? The life we live in gratitude to Jesus will show people just how much the gospel matters to us and to the world.

Returning to 2 Corinthians 5, the second section we're going to look at is verses 18-19.

> "All this is from God, who reconciled us to himself and gave us the ministry of reconciliation: that God was reconciling the world to himself in Christ, not counting people's sins against them. And he has committed to us the message of reconciliation."

In the wake of a great loss—a spouse, a child, a parent, or friend—people sometimes start foundations to support a cause close to the heart of the person they lost—school music programs, special education funds, homeless shelters, and countless other worthy and important causes. By doing this, those left behind are telling the world that because this cause was so important to the person they lost, they are willing to take on that cause as their own.

Jesus loved us enough to give up everything to come here to rescue us, to defeat our sin and restore our relationship with God. Jesus came to offer eternal life to everyone who would believe in and follow Him. He sacrificed everything, died, and was resurrected, and then He went back to His Father in heaven. But He left behind our marching orders. We don't have to guess what was and is important to Jesus. He plainly tells and shows us what was most important to Him. If we're willing to take on the causes of those we love here on earth after they are gone, how much more should we Christians be willing to take on the cause of Jesus Christ? The Vietnam veteran was willing to travel great distances to honor the man who saved his life. What are we willing to do?

The words from 2 Corinthians 5:18–19 tell us what Jesus wanted us to do. These verses are very specific: Jesus has given to us the *ministry and the message of reconciliation*. Reconciliation means to restore a friendship with another. Christ came here to restore our friendship with God. The story of how that friendship was broken—as well as God's promise to restore that friendship—is recorded in Genesis 3. There we learn that after Adam & Eve sinned, God placed a gate at the entrance to the garden, separating them from God. When Jesus uttered the words from the cross, "It is finished", that gate was reopened and once again a relationship with God was possible. That is the work of reconciliation that God has entrusted to us and to His church. To share this message - that friendship with God is again available because of what Jesus did on the cross. He fully paid the debt for all our sin.

When Jesus went back to heaven, He left to us the ministry and the message of reconciliation. It's our job now to tell people about Jesus, to share Him with those who haven't yet been restored to friendship with Him, about what He did and what He offers. This was why Jesus called those first followers to be fishers of people.

Shouldn't that be the most important thing to those who love Him? We are messengers with the best story ever. Shouldn't we share it with everyone?

Peter reminds us of our responsibility in 1 Peter 3:15: "But in your hearts revere Christ as Lord. Always be prepared to give an answer to everyone who asks you to give the reason for the hope that you have. But do this with gentleness and respect."

When Peter says to be prepared to give an answer to those who ask, he is reminding us that there will be people watching us, searching for meaning in their own lives, looking for the "eternity" that God "has set... in the human heart" (Eccles. 3:1). But before people will take the time to ask you about your faith, they need to see evidence of your faith. Peter challenges us—*expects* us—to live in such a way that people will notice something different about us and our priorities. Our faith needs to be something more than what we do inside the walls of our church or our homes. Our faith needs to be something we take with us wherever we go: to work, the golf course, the coffee shop, family reunions, vacations, or wherever else we find ourselves.

We must also acknowledge that while we all can affect those around us (our family, friends, neighbors, and/or coworkers), for most of us the opportunity to change the world beyond our own communities will be primarily through our finances because we are not physically able to go to the ends of the earth to share

Jesus with people who don't yet know him. This will be the primary focus of the next lesson on personal stewardship, but we want to point out that this passage from 2 Corinthians—this ministry and message of reconciliation—requires us to commit money to support the many ways Jesus' story is being shared around the world. There are many organizations whose ability to share the gospel and do the hard work of ministering to the hurting around the world depend on the funds they receive.

There's a missionary pastor who used to tell this imaginary story:

> One day Satan came to God and asked him, "God, now that Jesus has gone back to heaven, how are you planning on getting your message of salvation out to the whole world?" God responded, "My people will do it." To this Satan pushed God again, but God replied again, "My people will do it." To this Satan responded, "All right, but just suppose they don't do it?" And God said simply, "I don't have any other plan."

That is the reality for Christ-followers. Romans 10:17 says that "faith comes from hearing the message." Paul wants us to understand that someone must tell the story about Jesus before people can respond. That is our task: to tell the world about God's offer of forgiveness and eternal life through knowing and trusting Jesus. God has given us, His followers, the ministry of reconciliation. This reconciliation, restoring friendship between God and God's people, is what matters most to God.

Let's finish up this passage from 2 Corinthians 5 with the third and final section, verse 20.:

"We are therefore Christ's ambassadors, as though God were making his appeal through us."

Paul gets very personal here when he tells us that we are to be *ambassadors* for Christ. An ambassador is an official envoy, a high-ranking diplomat with a special task. In this letter to the Corinthians, Paul is challenging them (and us) to be agents of the highest rank, sent as representatives from God to the world with a special assignment. This special assignment is what Paul talked about in the previous verses: the ministry of reconciliation. But here Paul is even more specific when he explains that God intends to make His appeal to the world *through us*. Read that again. We are agents of the highest rank, sent on behalf of God himself to God's people living on earth to share with them God's offer of forgiveness and eternal life through Jesus Christ. The words "through us" leave no room for doubt about what God expects from us, and together as God's church, God's offer is our task to share.

One day God will surely ask me to give an account of my ambassadorship. That makes me think about what I would say. God is asking you, too, to be His ambassador—but if you are a follower of Christ, you don't really have a choice. Paul says you *are* Christ's ambassador. If you did have a choice, would you sign up for this job? Would you want to be—*do* you want to be—Christ's ambassador? If we're intent on being Christ's followers, we should. We should want to do it because Jesus' story is the best message, and because it's what Jesus asked us to do. We should want to do it out of gratitude to Jesus for defeating sin and death on our behalf. We should want to do it because our hope and our eternity are secure because of this reconciliation, and we should want to do it because so many people live apart from God and need to know that Jesus loves them so much He was willing to die for them.

In short, we should want to do it because the gospel really matters to us!

For further discussion:

- Name one thing in your life, your home, or your work that got you excited when it was new. How did that new thing affect you? Why?

- How does that new thing compare to being a new creation with Jesus? That might seem like a silly question, but why do these new things often affect us more than being a new creation? How can we turn that around?

- Read Acts 26. If you were standing before King Agrippa, what would your story be? Describe your "before" and "after" of knowing and being forgiven by Christ.

- Imagine a situation in which someone gave his life to save yours. How would that make you feel? How would you react?

- How could each of us show our commitment to this message of reconciliation? How could we show that the gospel really matters to us?

- Do you see the job of being an ambassador for Christ as a full-time or part-time position? If you answered "full time," how might God expect it to be full time when you have so many other jobs to fill?

- What does being an ambassador look like in your everyday life, in your daily routines? Would someone who works with you, lives with you, or is a friend to you know that this is a job you see yourself being asked to do? Why or why not?

- Imagine you are walking down a street and you see a house on fire. Flames are already consuming the roof. Inside you see a family sitting at the table, unaware of the fire. What would your reaction be? How would this compare to your reaction to knowing a family that has never heard the gospel or had a real opportunity to respond to it? Why is our reaction usually so different? What keeps us from responding to these two situations in the same way?

> *"How hard it is for the rich to enter the kingdom of God! Indeed, it is easier for a camel to go through the eye of a needle than for someone who is rich to enter the kingdom of God."*
> *— Luke 18:24-25*

LESSON 3

WHAT IS THE MATTER WITH MY GIVING?

From the last lesson we probably all can agree on *what* Jesus calls us to be as followers and *why* we should want to follow Him. Both the *what* and the *why* might have been pretty hard to swallow. Jesus does not ask us to do only easy and painless things here on earth. No, He asks us to do the difficult, the uncomfortable, and the costly things—just like He did. We're glad you're still with us on this journey. Apparently we haven't scared you off yet. That's the good news. The bad news is that the next step of this process may very well be the hardest one yet.

Our question for this lesson is: In light of my desire to be a follower of Jesus, what am I going to do about the issue of personal financial stewardship?

If you believe Jesus is calling you to be His ambassador, as we understood in the last lesson from 2 Corinthians 5 (we hope you said "yes"), you need to know what God expects from you when it comes to how you handle your money and other gifts.

In Matthew 6:24, Jesus makes a challenging statement: "No one can serve two masters. Either you will hate the one and love the other, or you will be devoted to the one and despise the other." The "other" here that Jesus is talking about is money. He says you cannot serve both God and money. Jesus singles out money as the greatest challenge for a Christ-follower—indeed, one of the greatest risks to our being ambassadors for Him. We have to be willing to ask and answer the question, "Am I going to follow God's plan for my life, or will I allow the desire for money and all it offers to direct my life?" Jesus is clear that you must choose between Him and money. It can't be both. To illustrate how deeply God feels about this, let's look at some additional passages from the Bible.

The first passage comes from the Old Testament, from Malachi 1:6-10, 13b-14. Read through this passage, and then answer the questions that follow.

> "A son honors his father, and a slave, his master. If I am a father, where is the honor due me? If I am a master, where is the respect due me?" says the Lord Almighty.
>
> "It is you priests who show contempt for my name.
>
> "But you ask, 'How have we shown contempt for your name?'
>
> "By offering defiled food on my altar.
>
> "But you ask, 'How have we defiled you?'
>
> "By saying that the Lord's table is contemptible. When you offer blind animals for sacrifice, is that not wrong? When you sacrifice lame or diseased animals, is that not wrong? Try offering them to your governor! Would he be pleased with you? Would he accept you?" says the Lord Almighty.

Giving that Matters to God

"Now plead with God to be gracious to us. With such offerings from your hands, will he accept you?"—says the Lord Almighty.

"Oh, that one of you would shut the temple doors, so that you would not light useless fires on my altar! I am not pleased with you," says the Lord Almighty, "and I will accept no offering from your hands.

"When you bring injured, lame or diseased animals and offer them as sacrifices, should I accept them from your hands?" says the Lord. "Cursed is the cheat who has an acceptable male in his flock and vows to give it, but then sacrifices a blemished animal to the Lord. For I am a great king," says the Lord Almighty, "and my name is to be feared among the nations."

- What is the basic message of this passage for a Christ-follower today?

- Read Leviticus 23:9–14. Compare God's instructions there for Israel's sacrifices and offerings to the practices being followed during the time of Malachi. What is the difference?

- This passage does not tell us what was behind the change in the sacrifices the people of God were offering, but what might be some of the reasons?

- Look again at God's words in the verse starting with "Oh, that one of you..." Rewrite God's reply in your own words—words that would apply to us today.

That response from God must have really shocked God's followers. The temple was the only place where the Israelites could meet with God. They went to the temple to pray, to hear teaching, to worship, and to offer sacrifices for their sins. When God tells them it would be better for them to shut the temple doors, God was telling them that all these temple activities mean nothing when you intentionally give God an offering that is not your best. It seems that if God were speaking to the church today, God would say, "You can have your Bible studies and your prayer meetings, and you can worship at church every week, but if you're giving me your leftovers for my work, then just shut the church doors because that won't matter to me."

Let's move now to another Bible passage. In the last chapter of 2 Samuel, we read about a time when King David had sinned against God by numbering the people of Israel to see how many soldiers he had even though God had instructed him not to do so. God was angry with David and sent a plague on all of Israel; many Israelites died. We pick up the story right after David had gone to God, repented, and asked for forgiveness. God heard David's cries and sent a man by the name of Gad with instructions for David (2 Sam. 24:18–25):

> On that day Gad went to David and said to him, "Go up and build an altar to the LORD on the threshing floor of Araunah the Jebusite." So David went up, as the LORD had commanded through Gad. When Araunah looked and saw the king and his officials coming toward him, he went out and bowed down before the king with his face to the ground.
>
> Araunah said, "Why has my lord the king come to his servant?"
>
> "To buy your threshing floor," David answered, "so I can build an altar to the LORD, that the plague on the people may be stopped."

Araunah said to David, "Let my lord the king take whatever he wishes and offer it up. Here are oxen for the burnt offering, and here are threshing sledges and ox yokes for the wood. Your Majesty, Araunah gives all this to the king." Araunah also said to him, "May the Lord your God accept you."

But the king replied to Araunah, "No, I insist on paying you for it. I will not sacrifice to the Lord my God burnt offerings that cost me nothing."

So David bought the threshing floor and the oxen and paid fifty shekels of silver for them. David built an altar to the Lord there and sacrificed burnt offerings and fellowship offerings. Then the Lord answered his prayer on behalf of the land, and the plague on Israel was stopped.

The lesson we learn from David here is quite simple. David understood that a sacrifice that cost him nothing would not please God. Sacrifice by definition means there must be a real cost involved. And that's the question we all face when we give to God's work: "Is what

I'm giving a sacrifice, or is it what's left over after I have taken all I want for myself?" That is what God looks at.

Our final passage comes from Mark 12:41–44:

> Jesus sat down opposite the place where the offerings were put and watched the crowd putting their money into the temple treasury. Many rich people threw in large amounts. But a poor widow came and put in two very small copper coins, worth only a few cents.
>
> Calling his disciples to him, Jesus said, "Truly I tell you, this poor widow has put more into the treasury than all the others. They all gave out of their wealth; but she, out of her poverty, put in everything—all she had to live on."

Jesus and his disciples were sitting in the temple at a spot where they could watch the temple goers deposit their offerings. Several people whom they knew were rich either by appearance or acquaintance deposited their sizable offerings. Then this widow took her turn. Just as the disciples were able to assess the wealth of the previous temple goers, they could tell that this woman was poor and alone. Yet she came into the temple area, went to the offering box, and deposited two small coins. Mark tells us the value of these two coins amounted to basically nothing, just a few cents.

What do you think the disciples were thinking when, after seeing the rich temple goers drop in their generous, sizable, and probably noisy offerings, this poor, lonely woman quietly approached the box and dropped in her meager contribution?

The disciples had to have been surprised by Jesus' words: "Truly I tell you, this poor widow has put more into the treasury than all the others." Obviously she did not literally give more than the others. Jesus explained that the rich gave out of their abundance while the widow gave out of her want. Jesus was clearly teaching that generosity isn't about how much you give; it's about what you keep for yourself.

There is so much contained in the three stories we've looked at. In Malachi, God tells the Israelites that it would be better for them to close the temple than to keep offering their blind, lame, and crippled sacrifices. In 2 Samuel, David refused to accept an offer of a free gift to make his sacrifice of repentance, saying, "I will not sacrifice to the LORD my God burnt offerings that cost me nothing." And then we read of the poor widow whose gift of mere pennies was heralded as a far greater gift than the sizable gifts from the wealthy men who came to the temple before her.

Let's take all these verses and apply them to ourselves today. What kind of giving does Jesus call us to today? What will make our gifts, our offerings, pleasing to God? These passages refer to a tithe, or ten percent of one's income and possessions. Is this still the standard to which we should be held? If not, what is the standard? If both the wealthy Jews in the temple and the widow had given ten percent, would that have pleased God? If not, why? What does God expect from us as God's followers, God's ambassadors? What is God asking of you?

Below is a list of facts and questions. Read through them, think about them, and answer the questions. Think about whether these descriptions reflect giving out of want (sacrificial giving) or giving out of our leftovers. Do these facts paint a picture of ambassadors and followers of Jesus? (Be prepared: some of these questions might step on your toes a bit. Try not to get defensive; just honestly evaluate these facts and questions.)

- Stewardship surveys indicate the average Christian gives about three percent of one's income to the church. That is about the same as what non-Christians give to charity.

- There seems to be a basic philosophy among Christians today that says if I can afford it I can have it. How does that philosophy fit with our discussion about offering God my leftovers? What are your criteria when deciding where you spend your money?

- Fifty years ago the average home had about 100 square feet per household member. Today that has increased to about 1,000 square feet per household member.

- Do the homes of Christ-followers today look any different from those of the world?

- If you looked inside the pole barns and garages belonging to Christ-followers, would there be fewer "toys" than in the garages of those who are not Christ-followers?

- If non-Christians observed what we Christians spend our money on, would it look any different from how they spend their money? Should it?

- Is there any monetary line you would set beyond which you would feel it's not okay for you to spend? If so, where is that line? Is it true that if someone is wealthy they deserve more things, bigger houses, fancier cars, bigger boats, more toys, or more vacations? Why or why not?

- If Jesus were watching you give money designated for his work, would he say you gave out of your abundance or your want? If you could see Jesus watching you give, would you give the same amount? Do you think he does watch?

"Give and it will be given to you; good measure, pressed down, shaken together and running over, will be poured into your lap. For with the measure you use, it will be measured to you." —Luke 6:38

Lesson 4

Giving That Matters

If you're still with us—if you haven't put the book down and thrown up your hands in despair, and if you're still willing to move forward on this journey of discovering how to be followers and ambassadors—great! Let's keep going.

We've made this topic of stewardship a two-part lesson. We think it is just that important and perhaps costs Christ-followers the blessing God really wants to give them more than anything else.

The question every Christ-follower needs to ask is this: Does my giving really cost me anything? If not, should we expect God to feel differently than in the stories we looked at in the last lesson? Perhaps we need to remind ourselves that God doesn't *need* our money. God doesn't sit in heaven like a beggar looking for a handout to enable Him to work here on earth. God will use others to accomplish His purposes if I choose to sit on the sidelines, but those "others" will receive God's blessing instead of me. The Bible is clear that God's kingdom needs must be first on our list when allocating our resources, not partway down.

Why is God so interested in our giving sacrificially? As we look at the words of Jesus, it becomes clear that there are real pitfalls for our ability to follow Jesus, our ability to take up his cause here on earth, if we don't have a godly perspective on money. It doesn't take much reading of the Bible to see what moves God's heart. The Bible shows us time and again how deeply God cares about people, the human race God so lovingly created and placed on this earth. The desire of God's heart is to have all people come to know Him and to be released from the pain and suffering that sin creates in their lives.

We see evidence of this in Luke 15. Jesus shares His heart for lost people by telling the stories of the lost sheep, the lost coin, and the lost son. (If you're not familiar with these stories, put this book down and read them so you can understand how much God cares about lost people.) Note that in each story great measures were taken to recover what was lost, and when it was found there was a great celebration. That is God's heart—every time one person who is lost is found, there is a grand celebration in heaven. We see God's heart again in John 3:16: "For God so loved the world that he gave his one and only Son." That is not a love that we find anywhere here on earth.

Jesus' last words to the disciples before going back to heaven (Matt. 28:18–20) have implications for our financial stewardship as well:

> "Then Jesus came to them and said, "All authority in heaven and on earth has been given to me. Therefore, go and make disciples of all nations, baptizing them in the name of the Father and of the Son and of the Holy Spirit, and teaching them to obey everything I have commanded you. And surely I am with you always, to the very end of the age."

It's hard to imagine how Jesus could have been clearer about what He expects from those of us who

Giving that Matters to God

call ourselves Christ-followers or from the organizations we call the church.

There are so many ways for all of us today to be part of sharing the gospel with both people in our own communities and those who live far away but are still part of God's family. God calls some to go to these faraway places to do His work. For some it means moving permanently to an area of the world where people need to hear about God's love for them. For others, short-term mission opportunities are a way to bring the gospel to those that are far away. For still others, their own communities and families are their mission field. Those are all valid and necessary ministries. But a way for all of us to participate in this work is given in Romans 10:12–15:

> "Everyone who calls on the name of the Lord will be saved." How, then, can they call on the one they have not believed in? And how can they believe in the one of whom they have not heard? And how can they hear without someone preaching to them? And how can anyone preach unless they are sent? As it is written: "How beautiful are the feet of those who bring good news!"

How can anyone preach unless they are sent? It makes perfect sense that mission work requires lots of "senders." God calls all of us to be senders. God asks all of us to support the work of sharing the gospel to the whole world. Supporting the work of evangelistic radio broadcasting, getting Bibles out in languages people can read and understand, giving financial support to families who choose to live and work in places away from home so they can reach people with the gospel message—these are all examples of mission work that require a few to go and a lot of people to send (and by "send" I mean "pay the bills and offer any other needed financial support). The amount of outreach God's people can accomplish by any means is almost directly related to the finances available. And there are literally billions of God's children who have not heard the gospel. We have the opportunity to change people's eternal destiny by committing to financially support the efforts of those who are bringing God's message of salvation to people around the world. And if we as "senders" are going to lean into God's command in Matthew to go into all the world, it can't be done with our leftovers, but only with a real commitment that costs us something—a sacrifice.

Another area of opportunity for how to direct our finances is described in Matthew 25:34–40. Jesus tells us here how much He cares for all the hurting people in the world, just as His heavenly Father does:

> "Then the King will say to those on his right, 'Come, you who are blessed by

my Father; take your inheritance, the kingdom prepared for you since the creation of the world. For I was hungry and you gave me something to eat, I was thirsty and you gave me something to drink, I was a stranger and you invited me in, I needed clothes and you clothed me, I was sick and you looked after me, I was in prison and you came to visit me.'

"Then the righteous will answer him, 'Lord, when did we see you hungry and feed you, or thirsty and give you something to drink? When did we see you a stranger and invite you in, or needing clothes and clothe you? When did we see you sick or in prison and go to visit you?'

"The King will reply, 'Truly I tell you, whatever you did for one of the least of these brothers and sisters of mine, you did for me.'"

In this passage we see Jesus' heart for the needy of the world. He goes on to say that if we neglect the hungry, the thirsty, and the sick, we are in essence neglecting Him. The needy could be our neighbor across the street or a child across the world. Jesus leaves no room for doubting how important these people are to Him. And there is no doubting that there are hurting and needy people in our world.

In his book *The Hole in Our Gospel*, Richard Stearns, the chief executive officer of the humanitarian agency World Vision, reminds us that thousands of children die every day from issues that could easily be prevented. UNICEF says 5.6 million children under five years of age will die this year from malaria, pneumonia, or other preventable causes. The Bible is very clear about how much God cares about children. In Matthew 19:14, Jesus says, "Let the little children come to me, and do not hinder them, for the kingdom of heaven belongs to such as these." The needs are so great and the means to help are readily available, yet all too often the church has looked the other way and used their available funds for purposes other than missions.

Jesus calls us to be His ambassadors, both by making God's appeal to people who do not know Jesus and by caring for those who are hurting, suffering, lonely, needy, abandoned, and helpless. This requires both our time and our money—two things that are not always easy for us to give. For most of us, the primary way we will serve as God's ambassadors requires our money. We concluded in an earlier lesson that just how much we believe the gospel matters will determine how we respond to this call.

Giving that Matters to God

There is no question that God has gifted some with monetary wealth. Clearly some have obtained wealth to a level far beyond what most of us are accustomed to. But if we compare ourselves (presumably North Americans) to the world, we are *all* wealthy (see *tinyurl.com/qb4gt8b*). Understanding this, I think some questions are important for us to consider:

- Did I create this wealth, or did God allow circumstances in my life that led to this wealth?

- How often do I think that circumstances totally outside of my control allowed my wealth to happen? These circumstances could include health, relationships, parents, the stock market, and more.

- If I think my wealth was accumulated because of my intellect, who gave me that?

- How much wealth can I keep for myself? How do I decide how many homes, how many cars, how many vacations, or how many shoes I should have?

- Did God give me this wealth to enjoy or to make a difference in God's kingdom?

- How does the phrase "to whom much is given much will be required" apply to the wealthy?

- There is a hymn we sing in church that says, "Take my life and let it be, ever only all for thee." Another line says, "Take my silver and my gold; not a mite would I withhold." How comfortable are you singing that verse?

When we look at Jesus' teaching in the Bible, it is easy to see that money was an important subject. He had more to say about money and its influence in our lives than about any other single topic. One cannot listen to Jesus without being aware of the fact that He saw money as a challenge to our relationship with Him. What is Jesus telling us in the following verses?

> **Mark 10:25** "It is easier for a camel to go through the eye of a needle than for someone who is rich to enter the kingdom of God"

> **Matt. 6:24** "No one can serve two masters. Either you will hate the one and love the other, or you will be devoted to the one and despise the other. You cannot serve both God and money"

Giving that Matters to God

Luke 12:13–21 "Someone in the crowd said to him, "Teacher, tell my brother to divide the inheritance with me."

Jesus replied, "Man, who appointed me a judge or an arbiter between you?" Then he said to them, "Watch out! Be on your guard against all kinds of greed; life does not consist in an abundance of possessions."

And he told them this parable: "The ground of a certain rich man yielded an abundant harvest. He thought to himself, 'What shall I do? I have no place to store my crops.'

Then he said, 'This is what I'll do. I will tear down my barns and build bigger ones, and there I will store my surplus grain. And I'll say to myself, "You have plenty of grain laid up for many years. Take life easy; eat, drink and be merry."'

"But God said to him, 'You fool! This very night your life will be demanded from you. Then who will get what you have prepared for yourself?'

"This is how it will be with whoever stores up things for themselves but is not rich toward God"

Luke 6:38 "Give, and it will be given to you. A good measure, pressed down, shaken together and running over, will be poured into your lap. For with the measure you use, it will be measured to you"

2 Corinthians 9:6-15 "Remember this Whoever sows sparingly will also reap sparingly, and whoever sows generously will also reap generously. Each of you should give what you have decided in your heart to give, not reluctantly or under compulsion, for God loves a cheerful giver. And God is able to bless you abundantly, so that in all things at all times, having all that you need, you will abound in every good work. As it is written:

> 'They have freely scattered their gifts to the poor; their righteousness endures forever.'

Now he who supplies seed to the sower and bread for food will also supply and increase your store of seed and will enlarge the harvest of your righteousness. You will be enriched in every way so that you can be generous on every occasion, and through us your generosity will result in thanksgiving to God.

This service that you perform is not only supplying the needs of the Lord's people but is also overflowing in many expressions of thanks to God. Because of the service by which you have proved yourselves, others will praise God for the obedience that accompanies your confession of the gospel of Christ, and for your generosity in sharing with them and with everyone else. And in their prayers for you their hearts will go out to you, because of the surpassing grace God has given you. Thanks be to God for his indescribable gift!"

Look again at the last three passages. Notice that in each of these God asks *us* to make the first move. Sacrificial giving is a faith venture. God promises that if we give to God, He will give back to us. The Bible is filled with promises of blessing for those who are faithful and obedient in stewardship. This blessing may not be monetary; in fact, many blessings from God are far more valuable than money. Why would we want to pass that up?

The question we all need to ask ourselves is this: "Does my giving cost me anything? Can I actually say there is something I really want that I'm giving up to promote the gospel? Or do I acquire everything I want and then give God what's left over?"

"Bring your offerings to God" says the Lord in Malachi 3:10, "and just see how many blessings God will pour out. That is God's challenge to each of us. Let's commit to taking one step at a time in expanding our stewardship and watch God work out His promisesin our lives. Are you in?

For further discussion:

- If you applied this lesson to your giving right now, what do you think God would say to you?

- In 2 Corinthians 9:6 Paul says, "Whoever sows sparingly will also reap sparingly, and whoever sows generously will also reap generously." Rate your sowing as either sparing or generous. Why did you rate yourself this way? How would God rate your giving? Why?

- What are three steps you could take to challenge yourself to better stewardship this month?

"I know your deeds, that you are neither cold nor hot. I wish you were either one or the other! So, because you are lukewarm—neither hot nor cold—I am about to spit you out of my mouth." —Revelation 3:15-16

LESSON 5

A CHURCH THAT MATTERS TO GOD

In the last lesson we looked at Bible verses that challenged us in our understanding of what God asks us to do in terms of our personal giving—our stewardship of the money God has entrusted to us. We heard God tell His people in the book of Malachi that if they were not being faithful in their giving they would be better off closing the doors of the temple. King David's story challenged us to make sure that our giving actually costs us something. And the poor widow showed us that it's not the amount given that pleases God; it's the sacrifice behind the gift that pleases God. That sacrifice means we are putting our trust in God rather than in ourselves—and that pleases God. Through all of these Bible passages and more, we learn that God doesn't want our leftovers. God wants us to give because we believe the gospel really matters and because we trust Him. These are some pretty high expectations.

These high expectations aren't just for our personal stewardship. God has those same expectations for His church; the community of believers that seeks to worship, obey, and serve Him. Look again at Malachi 3:10–12. Recall that God is speaking to people who have been offering Him blind or lame lambs for sacrifices and keeping the best for themselves. God accuses them of robbing Him, the maker of heaven and earth. Then, in verse 10, God challenges them with these words:

> Bring the whole tithe into the storehouse, that there may be food in my house. Test me in this," says the Lord Almighty, "and see if I will not throw open the floodgates of heaven and pour

> out so much blessing that there will not
> be room enough to store it.

It's easy to focus on the latter part of that passage, at God's promise to "open the floodgates of heaven and pour out so much blessing that there will not be room enough to store it." But we can't overlook the beginning, the prerequisite for God's blessing. This outpouring comes only after we "bring the whole tithe into the storehouse." Have you ever wondered what is the "storehouse" that is referred to here? Every Israelite at the time would have known this was the fund to provide for the workings of the temple. The question we need to answer is: has the storehouse (work) changed since Jesus gave His command to go into all the world and share the gospel?

In the Old Testament, God's work was primarily with the people of Israel, but it seems clear that this is no longer the case. Jesus' final command to His followers to go into all the world and preach the gospel to everyone means that God now extends His offer of love, forgiveness, salvation, and eternal life to all the people in the world.

God's work is not limited to just spreading the gospel. God calls the church, Christ's followers, to care about and for hurting people. In fact, Jesus tells us that failing to help the hurting is the same as not caring about Jesus. These tasks are what God's "storehouse" is today, not just for individuals, but for the community of believers—the church.

We often operate as if our churches have the same role and responsibilities as the Old Testament temple, but that is just not accurate. For the Israelites, the temple was the place they went to meet God. It was where they went if they wanted to be in God's presence. Today, pastors and churchgoers often mistakenly use the phrase "God's house" to refer to the building where we gather on Sunday for worship. It is our assertion that nothing has done more to hinder the church's ability to do mission work in the world than this misunderstanding of what God's house really is. This misunderstanding has stood in the way of Jesus' command to go into all the world with the gospel. Fancy church buildings and their maintenance are often the largest items in our church budgets and consume huge amounts of our financial resources. Successful fund drives to raise the money are touted as evidence of God's approval.

It seems obvious that both the martyr Stephen and the apostle Paul would have disagreed with the idea of a church building being God's house. They understood that God's house was not and is not a building. When Stephen faced stoning by the Sanhedrin he made clear that the God he was serving did not dwell in temples made by human hands (Acts 7:48). The apostle Paul echoed this truth in his speech to the people of Athens in Acts 17:24: "The God who made the world and everything in it is the Lord of heaven and earth and does not live in temples built by human hands." These two Christ-followers understood that, since Pentecost, God dwells not in a building but in the hearts of people changed by the gospel message (Rom. 8:9).

When Jesus was leaving the temple in Matthew 24:1–2, His disciples wanted him to notice the beautiful building, but Jesus seemed unimpressed, telling His disciples that the temple would soon be destroyed. He wasn't just saying that the actual stone building was going to be destroyed (though it was). He was also saying that after His death and resurrection, the temple building was not going to be needed in the same way any longer.

If we were to recast the words of God in Malachi 3 for a modern context, we might hear God saying something like this:

> Bring your offerings to the body of people serving and following Jesus Christ, that there may be funds available to do the work of my kingdom. Test me in this, says the Lord Almighty, and see if I will not throw open heaven and pour out so much blessing that you will be able to meet every need that comes your way.

Giving to the temple in the Old Testament was called tithing. Tithing is giving a certain percentage of one's earnings or possessions (usually ten percent) to one's local worshiping community. It's a symbolic acknowledgement that God has provided for me, so I will now give back a percentage to God. It's important to note that tithing does not carry the same meaning in the New Testament. As we discussed in the lesson about personal stewardship, Jesus no longer calls us to give a percentage; rather, he raises the bar and asks for sacrificial giving.

Our model for giving to God's kingdom "storehouse"— the church and other people or organizations living out Jesus' commands to share the gospel and bring help and hope to hurting people—should be more like that described in these New Testament passages:

> **Luke 6:38**, "Give, and it will be given to you. A good measure, pressed down, shaken together, and running over, will be poured into your lap. For with the measure you use, it will be measured to you."

> **2 Corinthians 9**:6, "Whoever sows sparingly will also reap sparingly, and whoever sows generously will also reap generously."

One role of the church and its leaders is to encourage and challenge us into faithful and sacrificial giving toward God's kingdom work. Who are the leaders in our churches? Certainly our pastors. God called them into these roles, and they have been trained to teach and to lead. But they are not the only ones in our churches who are called to lead. Most churches surround their pastor with a governing board, a council, or some other group of officers who serve and lead along with the pastor. In my church tradition, they are, in fact, the true leaders of the local church, overseeing the pastor and the congregation. They make formal commitments to lead the church as Jesus would have wanted.

There are also those who are neither pastors nor council members who can and should provide leadership in the church—people who have the skills, gifts, and passion to motivate and lead people. We churchgoers, we followers of Jesus, are called to play an active role in the church of Jesus Christ. None of us can be merely spectators of the church's work. We are followers (that requires action) and ambassadors (that entails responsibility).

Leaders in our churches need to continually and aggressively challenge its members to personal stewardship—and not just when the church isn't meeting its budget. Jesus talked about money more than any other subject; surely the church must talk about this issue more than we currently do.

Our church leaders must also challenge their congregations with a mission strategy based on Jesus' earthly ministry and commands, one designed to affect both their local communities and the world. They need to challenge church members with opportunities to reach lost people, help the hurting, and bring justice for the oppressed. They must continually make their congregations aware of the needs in their communities and in the world.

Church leaders must work to make all of us more aware that the needs of the world are great and that the need for financial giving is unlimited. They must challenge all who would be Christ-followers to be Christ's ambassadors to this hurting world. To do this effectively, leaders must show the people that their giving will really matter, that it will have a real impact in the world. Church leaders must remind us of the promise God made to those who rise to His challenge—the promise to open the gates of heaven and pour down such blessings that we could meet every need that comes our way. Who wouldn't want to be a part of that church? Can you even imagine a church so obedient to this call that the blessings from God are so abundant they hardly know what to do with them all?

Let's say for argument's sake that we are all on board with this concept, and that we are eager and ready to bring our financial gifts to the church. We are convinced that the gospel is important enough to sacrifice something so the work of Jesus can be done. The next thing we have to decide is how we'll spend those funds so they will do the most good. There is no shortage of needs in our world, no shortage of things that your group of people could choose to spend these funds on. Who decides when and where the money will be spent or distributed, and how are those decisions made?

We believe that to make good stewardship decisions, every church needs a committee totally committed to identifying the areas of greatest need and then sharing those needs with the church. This committee should identify not only places to support financially, but places where people can volunteer. Perhaps this committee could even establish new ministries to care for community and global needs. And this committee must share with the church the results of the work they are encouraging and supporting.

The committee's goal must be to create in the body of believers a real hunger to change the world in Jesus' name. Church ministry is not about making smarter Christ-followers who understand theology, but rather Christ-followers who have a lived theology, who want to be part of a body making a difference and doing God's work in the world.

For many of us who grew up in the church, putting our money in the offering plate felt like the end of our responsibility. We were not directly involved in deciding how the church would spend that money.

But as the ones who entrust our money to the church, isn't it our responsibility to be sure that as a body of believers we are being true to what Jesus called the church to be about?

The normal church budget process involves a group of deacons or designated persons entrusted with the task of developing the church budget. Their task is to determine the financial needs required for the operation of the church for the coming year. This process seems adequate for the items that have a fixed cost like salaries, utilities, insurance etc. This process, however, seems very inadequate to determine the church's obligation to the ministry needs in the world of sharing the gospel and helping the hurting. There are no fixed costs here. The needs are unlimited. For a few to decide for an entire group of people what they can and should give is simply not possible. There's another truth that could help us make the best decisions in this matter. We need to remember that every budget decision has two consequences: What will this expense do? and What else could this expense have done somewhere else? The task of developing a mission budget can only be done by challenging every person to discern what God is asking them to give to God's work. If the church does not individually challenge its members, it can only result in lost blessings. God has made clear He wants his followers to give.

As you learn more about how your church distributes and uses the money entrusted to it, as you consider getting more involved in this area yourself, and as you seek to make the greatest impact on the world around you, reflect on these questions, statements, and statistics:

- Pastors rarely preach about stewardship, and when they do it is often because the church's budget is running short. Why do you think this is? What keeps pastors from preaching on this topic more often?

- Leaders of mission organizations will tell you that many pastors and church leaders are afraid to encourage giving to missional causes because they think it will hurt giving to the church budget. What does this kind of thinking imply? Is there anything wrong with this kind of thinking? Why or why not?

- The largest projects in many churches are building projects, not mission projects. Have you ever been involved in a large fundraising campaign for a mission project? Has your church ever taken out a loan to do a mission project? Do either of these scenarios sound absurd? Why or why not?

- In many churches the largest budget items are building payments and maintenance of those buildings. Those costs often far exceed the mission part of the budget. Is that okay? How does your church's mission budget compare with other line items?

- Some surveys have shown that in most churches 97 percent of the money collected is spent in the local church, on ourselves, while only 3 percent goes to mission and ministry outside the church walls. Is that okay? Do you know what those percentages are for your own church?

- The same surveys asked why churchgoers gave only 3 percent of their income to the church. People said they felt as if their giving to the church never really made a difference in the community or the world. How does the church contribute to or prevent these kinds of perceptions?

- There are many who think the church is more focused on meeting the needs of the people inside the church than on the needs of those outside the church. What would you say to that?

- If you asked people in your congregation what the real purpose of their church is, what would they say? How would you answer that question? How many different answers would you get? If there are many different answers, what does that say?

- Jesus talked of laying up treasure in heaven. What do you think Jesus meant by "treasure"? In many churches today, it seems, those treasures are thought to be knowing more of the Bible, praying more, and attending church more. Are these the treasures Jesus was referring to, or are these supposed to be a means to the end of developing real ambassadors for Christ? What do you think are the treasures Jesus was referring to?

In *The Hole in the Gospel*, as we noted earlier, the author argues that the church has turned a blind eye to the needs of the world, including problems that are preventable yet still cause the deaths of thousands each day, many of them children. If you had to drive past groups of starving children on your way to a meeting to vote on a new church building project, would that affect your vote? It often seems that situations out of our sight are out of our minds. We once might have been able to excuse this by saying we didn't know how conditions were in other countries, but in today's world of instant communication and the internet that's no longer true. If we take the time to look, we can see images every day of abandoned or orphaned children, of deadly drought and starvation that plague so many countries and peoples, of places with no clean drinking water. We can no longer turn a blind eye. It's hard to imagine Jesus, if faced with a choice between a new building or thousands of dying children, coming down on the side of a new building, new carpeting, air conditioning, or a better parking lot. If Jesus would choose the children and their needs, can we do otherwise?

Have we Christ-followers conformed too much to the culture around us? Has it become too important for our church buildings to blend into the current stylistic trends as we do with our homes? Do we feel that in order to attract new people we need to *look* a certain way rather than *be* a certain way? Remember Jesus standing outside the beautiful and magnificent temple in Jerusalem and telling His disciples that not one stone of that magnificent temple would remain stacked on another. The building doesn't make the church. The hearts of the people make the church, and these hearts should be pushing the church to use the gifts given to God to make a real difference in God's world. We don't need to fit into our culture. I think Jesus would rather we stand out from our culture, both in our hearts and in how we spend our money. If the gospel really matters to us, do you think that our houses, our cars, our vacations, and maybe lots of other things should look different from those who don't profess to follow Jesus? I know that's a hard question to hear, and it may be even harder to answer. Jesus calls us to live differently, not as the world lives. But do our lives really look any different?

We think there is a common feeling that God is pleased with my church as long as we meet every Sunday, a pastor preaches a sermon, and we have enough resources to keep the lights on. But in the book of Revelation, the final book of the Bible, the resurrected and ascended Jesus tells John to transcribe letters to seven churches. Jesus obviously was aware of what was going on in these churches and in the hearts of the people in those places. These letters pointed out—sometimes in very painful and graphic terms—where most of these churches had fallen short and needed to change. It's clear from these letters that simply *being* a church is not satisfactory to Jesus. To one of those churches, he actually says, "I am about to spit you out of my mouth" (Rev. 3:16).

We know God wants His church to be successful. We know that God loves the church and is eager and willing to work through the church to change the world. I challenge you to read through these letters in Revelation 2 and 3. Then think about what God would say in a letter to your church. How might God encourage and challenge you? What strengths would God draw out? What would God say are your weaknesses or areas that need to change?

Look at what God says to the church in Ephesus in Revelation 2:4: "You have forsaken the love you had at first." It seems God is telling that church (and maybe your church too) that they have forgotten the basics of what God calls the church to be about. Jesus might be telling your congregation to go back to the heart of what being the church of Christ means. Is your church devoting its people and resources to the things that really matter to God? We can easily get sidetracked into thinking that our programs, our ministries, our presence on social media, our decor, our coffee and snacks before and after church, or hundreds of other good things are what the church is about. Take a step back, however, and examine if you and your church are really affecting the world we live in for Jesus. Are we being the church that Jesus asked us to be?

There is perhaps one simple idea that could produce real change in our churches. There was a time when we were all encouraged to wear a wristband that simply said WWJD, "What Would Jesus Do." Suppose that simple question was asked of each church leader before every major financial decision was approved. Jesus sees the world with all its needs, not just our church and our wants. Recognizing the money was given to do Jesus' work surely requires an answer to the question "What would Jesus do?" And the answers to this question might just lead the church to make very different decisions.

Our hope is that every church leader and church member would ask themselves and each other, "What is the purpose of my church?" We need to be sure the purpose we are pursuing is the purpose Jesus intended for His church. Once you come up with an honest answer for that question, check to see if your answer aligns with what Jesus laid out for His disciples. Are they similar? Do you need to adjust your answer? (I don't think we want to adjust Jesus' answer to fit ours.)

The model laid out by Jesus for His disciples offers us a guide. He called them by saying, "Come, follow me, and I will send you out to fish for people." That included worship, teaching, praying together, and practicing what they were learning. But we must also see that after three years of getting His disciples ready, the day came when Jesus told them to go and change the world. Our churches must be training centers designed to equip Christ-followers *to do ministry in the world*.

Church was never intended to be an adult education program where we spend a lifetime being taught with no expectation of using our learning to carry out the Great Commission. A church that simply has a Sunday service with all its finances going toward keeping the lights on cannot be what God expected of His church. When we devote our gifts to the mission of the gospel and ministry to those who are hurting, God will pour out blessings so bountiful that we won't know what to do with them all. Can you imagine what an impact that would have in the lives of both the people doing the giving and those on the receiving end of that giving? I know one thing for sure: I want to be a part of that kind of church. Don't you?

For further discussion:

- If we call the place we live "our house" or "my house" and then refer to our church buildings as "God's house," what might that imply? What do you think it communicates, intentionally or unintentionally, to people outside the church? Should we change how we refer to our church buildings?

- How long has it been since you've heard a sermon on stewardship? What do you remember about it? Was the sermon focused on needs in your church or needs in the world? Did it leave an impression? If you haven't heard a sermon on stewardship, why do you think your pastor hasn't tackled that subject?

- Have you ever been to a church meeting where people discussed and approved the church budget? Did you really look at where the money was being spent? Did you ask any questions or advocate for more mission spending? Do you feel as if you have some responsibility to determine how your gifts to the church are spent?

- If you have a copy of your church's budget, look at where the money is being distributed. How does it line up with what we've talked about in this chapter? If you could create the budget, what changes would you make?

We realize we have covered a lot of issues related to the organized church in this lesson. We know some of these issues are difficult, and many of our habits & traditions have been a part of our churches for a very long time. Change is not easy. Our goal is to help you think about stewardship in a new way. So we'll end this lesson with a hypothetical example of a church situation that can help us understand what leading the church in stewardship could involve:

Suppose some folks in your church want to improve the building's appearance, hoping to make it more attractive and get more people to come. This group thinks that you need more room after church to socialize, a better place for coffee and cookies after church. Let's say that this is a major project, the cost of which is projected to be $1 million.

Now suppose some other folks say they'd like to have the church sponsor a group of children in a developing country. They propose that the church sponsor 100 children for $38 each per month. (per World Vision) They are convinced that we can change the lives and the future of those children by providing health care, a good education, and clean water—and they will learn about Jesus! It will also change the children's families, who will hear the gospel as well. In many developing countries, 20 percent of children will die before they turn five years old. It is likely that of the 100 children to be sponsored, twenty would not survive without this sponsorship.

The total cost for this project would be $45,600 a year. The money for a $1 million building project could fund these 100 children for more than twenty years (without even taking in account any interest on the $1 million.)

- Which project would you choose if you were a church leader?

- If you asked all the leaders, "What would Jesus choose?", how would both those who said yes to the sponsorship project and those who said yes to the church building project respond?

- Try to imagine a reason Jesus might say I'd rather you spend the money on this church building project.

- Now suppose these 100 needy children lived in your community and you saw them every day. Do you think the building project proponents would still choose the building?

- If the 100 needy children were in your church—children from your congregation—do you think anyone would still want to renovate the building? If everyone chose the sponsorship program, what would that say to the congregation and to the community?

We hope this lesson will make all of us wrestle at least a little with what exactly it means to be the church of Jesus Christ. Does the budget of my church say we are more about meeting our own needs or the kind of needs that touched Jesus' heart? Maybe this lesson will prompt you and other leaders in your church to ask more often this simple question: What would Jesus do?

> *I will build My church, and the gates of Hades will not overcome it.*
> *—Matthew 16:18*

LESSON 6

CAN YOUR CHURCH MATTER?

We all want to be a part of *that* church—you know, the one people in your town know about and notice serving around the community. The one where people are excited and eager to be a part of something bigger than themselves. So what's standing in our way? Why aren't we that church? How can we become that church? Can our church be the kind of church that really matters, a church that affects people's lives both inside and outside the building?

This lesson is for churches of all sizes, but especially the small churches often found in rural areas but certainly also in some city neighborhoods. This is the kind of church where everyone knows everyone else, and church is mostly about fellowship with other Christians. It's the church where we have hardly enough finances to pay a pastor and keep the lights on. We don't think about changing the world; we just want to stay alive as a church. For that church, the most important question might be: Can my church matter?

First we must understand how Jesus viewed the church (or, at the time of his ministry, the temple or synagogue). The church was not designed to be a social club, but rather an offensive, world-changing organization. Jesus said to Peter in Matthew 16:18, "I will build my church, and the gates of Hades will not overcome it." Have you ever wondered how strong the gates of Hell would have to be to withstand the attack of your church?

"Church" was not first and foremost about meeting together once a week for teaching and fellowship. It was really about what the church did the rest of the week. It was about how God-fearing people would interact with others. If you read through the gospels, it doesn't take long to see that how Jesus interacted with people—*all* people—was not what most people expected.

Individuals in the church cross paths with different people in different places every day as we go about our week. Each interaction is an opportunity to be the church, to be what Jesus intended us to be, to act like He did. This in no way depends on the size of your church. Every day we have the chance to distinguish ourselves in the world, to show people that our priorities are different. So let's make sure that our business dealings look different, that how we work and treat our coworkers and customers looks different. Let's make it clear to all that we have a different set of values that include honesty and integrity. Let's make sure that when we interact with those we meet at the coffee shop, the golf course, the office, the grocery store—wherever we find ourselves—that people around us notice a difference. Maybe they'll even ask you about it!

But we also need to understand that every congregation has hurdles that hinder its progress and effectiveness. We all want our churches to matter. But what are you willing to do, what obstacles are you willing to overcome, to make sure that your church does matter? The path for each church is different; there are no one-size-fits-all programs or strategies. But if your church really *wants* to matter, it absolutely can.

In the gospel of John we find this very familiar verse (John 3:16): "For God so loved the world that He gave his one and only Son, that whoever believes in Him shall not perish but have eternal life." God loves everyone in the whole world. He wants the church to reach all people. I think it is also God's desire that each church, no matter its context, regularly asks this important question: Where can *we* make a difference today in the world? When a church asks itself that question, seeks to answer it honestly and faithfully, and then actively searches out opportunities in its unique setting, it will be well on its way to becoming a church that really does matter.

How do we do that? Where do we do that? Do we focus on the people in our own communities; people we rub shoulders with at the gas station, the grocery store, and school events, neighborhood people who are hurting and need Jesus in their lives? Or people who live in those faraway places we see on TV or on the internet, families torn apart by war, poverty, AIDS, and human trafficking? I think we all know the answer to this question. It's not an either/or question. It's a both/and question. The answer is "yes"—to both groups.

Answering "yes" to both of these priorities presents us with a daunting reality. How do we make an impact not just on the community around us (which can be daunting in itself), but on the world? Where and how do we begin?

As we suggested in the last lesson, every church needs to have a group of dedicated, mission-minded people who can seek opportunities for the church to make a difference and then advertise them to the congregation. These opportunities need to be valid and varied. Different causes will appeal to different people and their different gifts. Having a group on the lookout for these opportunities that also has a good understanding of what people in your church are looking for would be a win for everyone.

At the same time, every congregation needs leaders to cultivate the desire to be a church that makes a difference in the world. If any one of us were to come face to face with a child in desperate need, I believe none of us would walk away unwilling to help. Yet thousands of children die every day because no one is there to help them. How do we change that? The answer certainly involves connecting church members with real needs and then seeing the effects that meeting those needs can have. Be sure to give frequent updates about how and where the church is doing this work effectively to inspire others to join in!

At some point, of course, we need to quit talking about having an impact in our world and actually start doing something toward that end. We need to find the people in our churches who are passionate about changing the world, both locally and globally. We need to identify key people willing to provide leadership in this effort. Once they have been engaged, they can get to work finding the things that will touch the hearts of the people in your church. This doesn't have to be rocket science. There are many easy and obvious places to start.

We want to leave you with a list of opportunities we know can have a real impact in our world. This list is just a small taste of what's out there for your church. Perhaps at least one of these will spark an interest in you and your group or be a springboard for finding other opportunities that will work for people in your setting. You just have to get started, take the plunge, try something new! God will use you to change lives—one of which most certainly will be yours!

- World Vision and Compassion International partner people with children all over the world to sponsor their health care, education, and basic food and clothing needs as well as to share the gospel with them, all for about $38 a month per child (per World Vision). A recent study measuring the effectiveness of these child sponsorship programs showed that adequate health care, education, food, and shelter, plus hearing the gospel, had a tremendous impact not only on the future of the sponsored child, but also on their entire family and even the community they lived in. Imagine if your church set a goal to sponsor one child for every family in your church. What an impact your church would have!

- There are several organizations, like Words of Hope, that broadcast the gospel by radio and over the internet to some of the most difficult to reach areas in the world. These broadcasts are often the only means that people have to hear the gospel message. These organizations depend on donations and your church could have a direct impact on spreading the gospel to people who otherwise would not hear it. These broadcasts also bring hope and encouragement to Christians facing persecution all over the world. Could your church adopt a small country - partnering with someone like Words of Hope to provide the gospel message to those living there?

- Unclean drinking water is one of the biggest causes of child deaths in the world. For around $5,000 you can sponsor a well in an area of desperate need. What if your church decided they would support one well placement every year? That single well would affect a whole community. Imagine how many lives your church could affect over ten years!

- Unemployment is rampant in most developing countries. There are not enough businesses for people to find employment and thereby support their family. What is needed are small enterprises like farming and selling vegetables, making jewelry, or sewing clothes. Many organizations provide start-up loans or grants for such small businesses. Your church could sponsor one of these projects. In India, for example, an agency will provide a sewing machine if someone first completes a training program where they will learn to sew and also hear the gospel. Each sewing machine costs the agency $108, a gift you can give that not only gives someone a livelihood supporting their whole family, making it possible for their children to attend school, but it also introduces them all to Jesus. How many sewing machines could your church provide?

- In places where Christianity cannot be practiced openly, many come to know Jesus in house churches. Many of these groups are led by new Christian lay pastors who don't even have a Study Bible, much less theology training. You can put a Study Bible in the hands of one of these pastors for only $37.

- Many of these same house church pastors live on a salary of less than $100 a month. Could your church support one or more of these pastors who often risk their lives sharing the gospel?

- We are not all able to go overseas to do hands-on mission work, but what about sending your pastor or a church leader to a developing country where they can see firsthand the needs and maybe connect with a family or families that your church could "adopt" and support? Imagine your church having families all over the world that you are connected with and can see God working through!

- In areas that are not open to missionaries, there are opportunities to purchase and distribute radios that can connect people with the gospel. They are powered by hand cranks or solar power and cost about $40 each. Just one of these radios can bring the gospel to a whole village of people.

- Every community, whether rural or urban, has unique needs. Putting the right people on the job to determine those needs and making them known to your church could have a huge impact right in your own community. Some of those needs might be child care for working families or transportation to and from jobs.

- Love INC has chapters all over the U.S. that coordinate services including food pantries, baby pantries, bed ministries, and other supply closets to help meet the needs of people in your community. See if there is a local chapter that your church could partner with - time and financial support would go a long way towards making your church matter in your community.

- Making a positive difference in your own community requires making connections with the people in your community. Start conversations with people you come into contact with throughout the week. As you do that, you will learn firsthand of the needs people in your area face every day. Get involved in community activities outside the walls of your church. Coach youth sports; assemble a pickleball, basketball, softball, or cornhole team that meets and plays regularly; go for a walk around town and introduce yourself to your neighbors; have a block party. The list of ways to engage your neighbors is endless, but you get the idea. Jesus interacted with all kinds of people He encountered on his journey. He's asking us to do the same.

In addition to these smaller or individual projects, we challenge your congregation to commit to one large project through which your church can enter into a long-term relationship with people either inside or outside your immediate community—a project you can regularly contribute to, get updates from, and even visit. Then invite people involved with that project to come to your church to share what's been going on.

Developing this kind of relationship with others in common support of a project will let your church experience firsthand the effect that their gifts are having. They will be able to hear the stories of lives changed and hearts touched. They will be able to see how God can and does use them to affect the world in mighty ways. Imagine if the conversations over coffee after church could be less about football games and the weather and more about lives being changed because of what your church is doing!

We all can be a part of *that* church. Your church can be the one that people know about and see serving the community, the one where people are excited and eager to be a part of something bigger than themselves. Remember that Jesus notices your church, and what He sees is really up to you.

For further discussion:

- Would you categorize your church as small, medium, or large?

- On a scale of 1 to 10, with 10 being the most, how much do you think your church matters to the world around you, both locally and globally?

- If Jesus were to write a letter to your church, what things would he highlight or draw your attention to? List some positive things and some things that need work.

- What are some areas of mission your church is currently involved in? What are some additional areas that might interest you?

- If you can't come up with any areas of mission that your church is currently involved in, how does this make you feel? What does this say to you about your church? How could you facilitate change in this area?

- Try looking at your church through Jesus' eyes. What makes your church different from the local country club? What is the conversation about as you meet over coffee and cookies after church? What would people in your community say about your church? Would Jesus see your church as a place of comfort or challenge? Try to compile a list of things that Jesus would applaud about your church. Then make a list of things that Jesus might challenge you to change or simply improve. What are some things that YOU could do to work on these areas that need attention?

Now to him who is able to do immeasurably more than all we could ask or imagine...
—Ephesians 3:20

LESSON 7

RISK-TAKERS MATTER TO GOD

Stewardship, as we have been learning, is really about taking a risk for God. It's about giving away what the world says is most valuable: our money. It's about taking a risk and believing that doing what God asks us to do, even when it's hard, will actually matter to God.

We started this study by looking at the question "What does it mean to follow Jesus?" Have we really considered what we signed up for when we decided to follow Jesus? As we come to the end of this study, we wonder if the lyrics to "I Have Decided to Follow Jesus" mean something more to you than they did when we started? We hope so. Following Jesus is not easy. He never promised that it would be. He actually promised the opposite.

As we wrap up our discussion of stewardship, we're going to turn to an amazing but somewhat troubling story found in Matthew 25. Jesus describes three people who were entrusted with different amounts of money (in units called "talents" in Jesus' time). When the master returned, he asked each one to give an account of what they did with the money they were given. The first one had invested and doubled his five talents, and the master commended him. The second had only two talents, but he too had invested and doubled his money, and the master commended him as well. The third one, who had been given only one talent, hid it in the ground because he was afraid that if he invested it he might lose it. The master took that talent from him and gave it to the first servant. What do you think was the point Jesus was trying to make?

It seems that playing it safe is not God's idea of being an obedient servant.

Hebrews 11 is known as the "Heroes of Faith" chapter. Look at the people listed there. If some of the names or stories are not familiar to you, go back and read their stories. Do you see a common thread in each of their stories? What do Noah, Abraham, Joseph, Moses, Rahab, Gideon, Samson, David, and all the rest share? They all trusted God and were willing to take big risks for God. The New International Version of the Bible even titles Hebrews 11 as "Faith in Action"!

Moses was willing to give up a life of luxury in Pharaoh's palace, choosing instead to lead God's often obstinate people across a hot and dusty desert. Abraham was willing to leave his home country and everything he knew for a new land. Joseph was willing to turn down a salacious offer from his master's wife even though it sent him to prison. Rahab was willing to risk her life to hide Israelite spies. It was a strong faith in God that prompted them to be risk-takers, to do what God called them to do no matter how hard or even impossible it might have seemed.

Look at Hebrews 11 again and think about the following questions:

- Describe the different kinds of people listed here. What does that teach us?

- Describe the kinds of risks they were asked to take. What can that teach us?

- God didn't ask them all to risk the same thing or even the same kind of thing. Some of the risks seem easier than others. What might we learn from that?

- What were some of the consequences of their risk-taking? Are the results similar to each other or not? What lesson is there for us?

As we sing (or simply say; for some of us that's the better way to go!) the words "I have decided to follow Jesus, no turning back, no turning back," are we willingly signing up to be risk-takers for God? Knowing that we will make mistakes along the way, are we willing to put aside our plans and our ideas to live instead by faith in the great God of the universe and take those risks for Him and His purposes?

There's a story in the Bible about twelve spies selected by Moses to scout the land of Canaan and its inhabitants to see what they were going to be up against. This was the land God had promised would be the Israelites' new home. They had traveled through the desert and endured all kinds of hardships to finally be at the edge of the land God was going to give to them. In Numbers 13:17–20, Moses sends off the twelve spies with the following instructions:

> "Go up through the Negev and on into the hill country. See what the land is like and whether the people who live there

are strong or weak, few or many. What kind of land do they live in? Is it good or bad? What kind of towns do they live in? Are they unwalled or fortified? How is the soil? Is it fertile or poor? Are there trees in it or not? Do your best to bring back some of the fruit of the land."

When the twelve returned, ten of them gave this report (Num. 13:27–28, 31–32):

"We went into the land to which you sent us, and it does flow with milk and honey! Here is its fruit. But the people who live there are powerful, and the cities are fortified and very large... We can't attack those people; they are stronger than we are... The land we explored devours those living in it. All the people we saw there are of great size."

Keep in mind these ten spies were believers in God. They had heard the stories and seen first-hand how God had rescued them over and over again. They had seen God defeat armies and pave the way to bring them to this new land. Yet in the face of the obstacles they saw in Canaan, they got scared. They couldn't see a way to defeat the Canaanites, and they must not have believed that their God was big enough to defeat them either. Their faith in God wavered, and their ability to take a risk and trust God dissolved. God made it clear that He wouldn't use people that wouldn't trust Him enough to follow even when it was risky. Because of the fear shown by these 10 spies, the rest of the Israelites were afraid too. The fear and lack of trust in God meant Israel had to wander in the desert for forty more years until they died, never getting to enter the land God had promised them.

Do you think some churches today are kept from experiencing the blessings God wants to give them because their leaders are afraid of taking risks in God's work? Maybe the majority of the people sitting in the pews are too afraid?

Back to the story: There were two spies who actually stood up to contradict the other ten. In Numbers 14:7–9, Joshua and Caleb said,

> "The land we passed through and explored is exceedingly good. If the Lord is pleased with us, he will lead us into that land, a land flowing with milk and honey, and will give it to us. Only do not rebel against the Lord. And do not be afraid of the people of the land, because we will devour them. Their

protection is gone, but the Lord is with
us. Do not be afraid of them."

Joshua and Caleb were willing to put their trust in God and take that risk. Perhaps in their minds it didn't even seem like a risk. They too had seen what God could do and had witnessed God's strength and care for His people. They knew that God is faithful to His promises. It didn't matter that the task looked impossible. It didn't matter that they probably had no idea how they would defeat such intimidating people. It only mattered that God had promised to help them. That was enough.

Now look at Ephesians 3:20–21, where Paul writes:

"Now to him who is able to do immeasurably more than all we ask or imagine, according to his power that is at work within us, to him be glory in the church and in Christ Jesus throughout all generations, forever and ever! Amen."

I think it might be impossible for us to really grasp the full potential of these words. Think of the greatest mission project you can imagine. What would that look like? Who would be involved? Where would you go? What would you do? What might the impact be of this project? Now go read that verse from Ephesians again. Whatever you can imagine, no matter how big or difficult, God can do immeasurably more than that! The people listed in Hebrews 11 could attest to that. Abraham wanted one son; he got descendants that numbered more than the stars in the sky. Joseph wanted to get out of prison and see his father; he not only got to do that but became second in command of all of Egypt. God is not limited by our imaginations. God doesn't want us to be limited by them either. God wants us to let Him do the imagining; we only must do the "following in faith" part. Can we set aside our fears, our doubts, and our human constraints to take those faith-filled steps with God?

Do you think God has ever said about you, "I can't believe he/she was willing to follow me there!" or "I can't believe he/she was willing to do that for me!" Do you think God has ever said these things about your church? Have we ever surprised God with our faith? Like the servant who risked the talents given to him by his master and doubled them, I know we want God to say to us and to our churches, "Well done, good and faithful servant! You have been faithful with a few things; I will put you in charge of many things. Come and share your master's happiness!" (Matt. 25:23).

Being risk-takers for God is at the very heart of stewardship. When God first made a covenant with His people, the Israelites, God asked them to bring Him their firstfruits as sacrifices. We've talked a lot about that already, but it bears repeating here. The firstfruits were what was gathered at the first harvest. The first harvest was the surest and often the best. There was no guarantee that the second or remaining harvests would be as fruitful, so sacrificing the firstfruits was a true exercise in trust. In surrendering their firstfruits to God the Israelites declared that they trusted God to provide what they needed to survive. We don't actually bring our first harvest of produce to God today, but God still asks us to give our first and our best. God asks us to give up what the world counts most valuable thereby trusting that God will provide for us and bless our commitment. Remember those words from Malachi? God challenges us to test Him so we can see that if we give generously God will "pour out so much blessing," more than we know what to do with!

We need to understand, however, that this is not a "prosperity gospel," a promise that if we give God money He will make us financially rich in return. Rather, God promises *God's* blessing, a blessing beyond our capacity. This won't always or even often come in the form of money. While God can certainly choose to bless his followers financially, the things that matter most in our lives are not money and possessions, but rather our families, our health, our relationships, and opportunities. God's economics are so different from the world's. God tells us that it's through losing that we find, through giving away that we receive, and through giving up that God gives back.

We discussed in a previous lesson how God's work for the church is laid out in 2 Corinthians 5. We are to be "Christ's ambassadors," bringing God's message and ministry of reconciliation and healing to the world. Are you willing to risk yourself in that effort? Are we as a church, a body of believers, willing to risk ourselves to step into a ministry, into a region, into a hurting part of God's world and make a difference? Is God currently challenging you (or us) with an opportunity for you, your family, or your church to make a difference? Are you being challenged to reach lost people or to help the hurting locally or globally? Are you reluctant to take the risk that this endeavor requires? God doesn't ask you to make a giant step all at once. Just take one step of faith in the direction that God is calling you and see what He does.

If you're reading this and still struggling with your ability to take these risks, read on. God doesn't expect things from us without giving us some important and helpful tools.

Earlier we looked at Ephesians 3:20–21, in which we're told that God is "able to do immeasurably more than all we ask or imagine." Let's back up and read the verses just before this, Ephesians 3:17–19:

> "And I pray that you, being rooted and established in love, may have power, together with all the Lord's holy people,

> to grasp how wide and long and high and deep is the love of Christ, and to know this love that surpasses knowledge—that you may be filled to the measure of all the fullness of God."

This prayer of Paul's for the followers of Jesus is what we need to remember as we face the fear and doubts that come along with steps of faith and situations that require us to take risks for God. Paul so earnestly wants the followers of Jesus to know how wide, long, high, and deep the love of Christ Jesus is for them. Paul, quite a risk-taker himself, understood that if we could grasp this truth, if we could grasp just how much God loves us and wants to bless us, those steps of faith and risks wouldn't seem so formidable. If we feel that love from our God, the creator of all that we know, we are more able to let go of our self-imposed limitations and trust that God will take care of things. If we believe that God loves us that much—and God does—it will be easier to trust that God is able to do far more than we can ask or imagine—and He will!

We are confident that if we follow God's leading, we will never look back and regret taking a risk for God. Don't let yourself play it safe and miss out on what God wants for you.

I'm reminded of a plaque that hung on a wall in the home I grew up in. It read, "Only one life will soon be past; only what's done for Christ will last." Those words are a good summary of what we've talked about. Now let's focus on the words of Jesus, glue your eyes to them, don't look back, don't doubt God, keep your path headed straight towards Him and follow Him!

For further discussion:

- What did you learn from the parable of the servants entrusted with talents (money) from their master? Which servant do you think you are most like?

- Reread the story of the twelve spies in Numbers 13–14. The ten spies who were not willing to risk moving forward with the plan to take over the promised land were believers in God. Have you ever thought of them as weak in their faith? After evaluating your own history of stepping out in faith—or of risk aversion—does this story strike you differently?

- As you look back over your life, are there any situations that you believe could have gone better if you had trusted God more? Do you think that having faith automatically makes you a risk taker? Why or why not? If not, what would you need to do to become more of a risk taker for God? Once you've identified these steps, share them with at least one other person. Ask that person to keep you accountable to following through with these steps.

- Have you ever done something that would make God say, "I can't believe you dared to do that!" Do you know of anyone else that would have done something to elicit that kind of response from God?

- Consider keeping a journal to keep track of the steps you're making to become a risk taker and how God blesses you because of those risks. We would love to hear your stories of risks taken and blessings poured out!

- Have you ever had a wish for yourself, your family, or your church that you really wanted but felt it was too big for you to tackle? What stood in the way of your trying? What would have to happen before you would try now?

You've made it to the end of this study. Looking back, what challenged you the most? Have you felt God nudging (or all-out pushing) you to make a change? If so, where? What might be some first steps that you could take to step into this change that God is leading you to? If this change that God is nudging you toward is directed toward your church, what might the first steps be to get that ball rolling?

As you finish answering these final questions, close this book and move on to the next thing on your schedule, it is our sincere hope and prayer that this book and the ideas presented in it don't end up like many other study books—collecting dust on a bookshelf. We hope and pray that the challenges that we have experienced and then shared with you in this book have moved you to a new place—perhaps an uncharted place with God, a place of trust, risk-taking, and a willingness to do one of the hardest things - change. We know that change is hard, and changing how you look at your money is maybe the hardest. But, as I tell my kids all the time, just because something is hard doesn't make it wrong. We know in our hearts that these challenges—the challenges that Jesus himself laid out for us while he walked this planet—are right. We know deep down that the needs of this world should win out over our own desire for more and better things. So step out of the norm, step out of what the world says is right and deserved, and step into being an active and eager follower of Jesus. The rewards for doing this are too great and too numerous to list. That's the promise that Jesus gives us, and those promises—they are like money in the bank.

Conclusion

We want to thank you for the time you have spent with us reading and studying these pages. Having traveled to developing countries and seeing the enormous needs of people all over the globe—needs that often have relatively easy fixes—we felt compelled to write this study. We saw places where one well could provide clean water, changing the future of a whole village, places where a basic vaccination could change the future of a child, places where a simple sewing machine could impact a family's future, and places where medicine to cure a child of malaria can save that child's life. We've seen the ravages of war and HIV/AIDS with dire consequences for children and entire villages. Perhaps you've seen or experienced some of these yourself. And then we remember these words of Jesus: "Let the little children come to me, and do not hinder them, for the kingdom of heaven belongs to such as these" (Matt. 19:14). And we realize that so many of these children, so many of these villages, will live and die never having heard that Jesus loves them. Their whole world is day to day survival without even imagining a tomorrow. But in today's world we can reach almost everyone with new technologies. All that limits us are the funds to do it. There are really two things standing in the way of changing thousands and perhaps millions of lives. The first is a misunderstanding of personal Christian stewardship that not only limits God's work but also the personal blessing God has promised. The second is that so many churches have looked the other way from the needs in the world and have focused instead on our wants. This is why we wrote this study. We are not authors; we are farmers and teachers. Our words in this study may be more direct than the Bible studies you are used to. But we hope you will sense how much stewardship matters to us. We believe it can change our lives, our churches, and the people God cares for all around the world. We pray that God might use this study to challenge you. Jesus said, "If anyone causes one of these little ones to stumble... it would be better for them" to die (Matt. 18:6). We can only assume Jesus would also say, "God will never forget someone who changes the life of a child." Could that person be you?

If God has touched you through this study and moved you to step out in faith to make a difference in this world for Jesus, we would love for you to share your story with us. You can email us at either of the

Conclusion

addresses below. We are confident that God will do mighty things through His followers.

In service to our great God,
Betsy Arkema   Wendell Van Gunst
betsy@countrydairy.com wendy@countrydairy.com

CPSIA information can be obtained
at www.ICGtesting.com
Printed in the USA
LVHW080052280221
680113LV00013B/1306